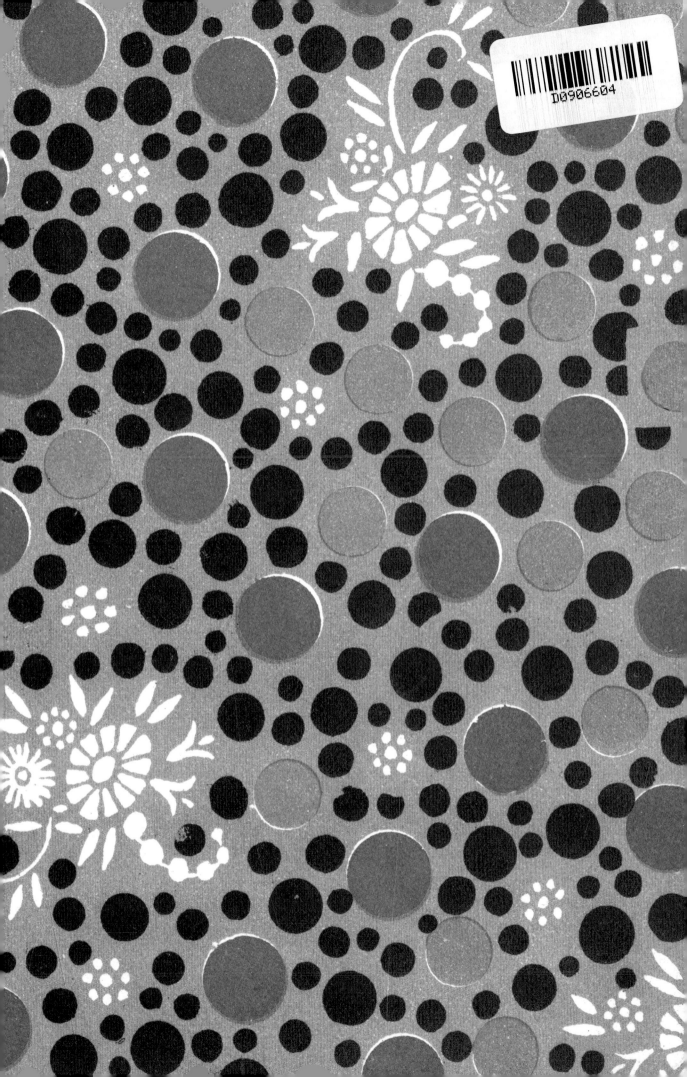

D0906604

with love

TO

FROM

I love you

POEMS OF LOVE

LAUGHING ELEPHANT • MMX

Bruton Memorial Library
Plant City, Florida 33563

PICTURE CREDITS

Cover: Gustav Klimt. "The Kiss", 1907.
Frontispiece: Dudley Tennant. From *Poems of Passion and Pleasure*, 1912.
Copyright: W. Heath Robinson. From *How To Live in a Flat*, c. 1932.
Page decorations: Margaret Armstrong
4: Edmund Dulac. From *Rubáiyát of Omar Khayyám*, 1909.
6: David Robinson. Magazine cover, 1925.
8: Henry J. Soulen. Magazine cover, 1922.
10: Warren Davis. Magazine cover, 1925.
12: John Cecil Clay. Magazine cover, 1912.
14: Dudley Tennant. From *Poems of Passion and Pleasure*, 1912.
16: Harold von Schmidt. Magazine illustration, 1941.
18: Edmund Dulac. From *The Poetical Works of Edgar Allan Poe*, c. 1912.
20: Claude Emil Schuffenecker. "Couple at Table," 1886.
22: Neysa McMein. Advertisement, c. 1917.
24: Jessie M. King. "Love's Golden Dream," c. 1914.
26: John Duncan. "Tristan and Isolde," 1912.
28: Edwin A. Georgi. Advertising illustration, c. 1932.
30: Edward Burne-Jones. "Love Among the Ruins," 1894.
32: Heinrich Comploi. From *Love Songs by Heinrich Heine*, c. 1910
34: Georges Rochegrosse. Poster, 1900.
36: Leon Kroll. "Spring Romance," n.d
38: Marianne. From *Les 6 princesses*, n.d.
Back Cover: Unknown. Advertising illustration, c. 1941.

COPYRIGHT © 2010 • LAUGHING ELEPHANT BOOKS

ISBN13 978-1-59583-383-9

FIRST PRINTING • ALL RIGHTS RESERVED • PRINTED IN CHINA

www.LAUGHINGELEPHANT.com

I love you

POEMS OF LOVE

LAUGHING ELEPHANT • MMX

Bruton Memorial Library
Plant City, Florida 33563

PICTURE CREDITS

Cover: Gustav Klimt. "The Kiss", 1907.
Frontispiece: Dudley Tennant. From *Poems of Passion and Pleasure*, 1912.
Copyright: W. Heath Robinson. From *How To Live in a Flat*, c. 1932.
Page decorations: Margaret Armstrong
4: Edmund Dulac. From *Rubáiyát of Omar Khayyám*, 1909.
6: David Robinson. Magazine cover, 1925.
8: Henry J. Soulen. Magazine cover, 1922.
10: Warren Davis. Magazine cover, 1925.
12: John Cecil Clay. Magazine cover, 1912.
14: Dudley Tennant. From *Poems of Passion and Pleasure*, 1912.
16: Harold von Schmidt. Magazine illustration, 1941.
18: Edmund Dulac. From *The Poetical Works of Edgar Allan Poe*, c. 1912.
20: Claude Emil Schuffenecker. "Couple at Table," 1886.
22: Neysa McMein. Advertisement, c. 1917.
24: Jessie M. King. "Love's Golden Dream," c. 1914.
26: John Duncan. "Tristan and Isolde," 1912.
28: Edwin A. Georgi. Advertising illustration, c. 1932.
30: Edward Burne-Jones. "Love Among the Ruins," 1894.
32: Heinrich Comploi. From *Love Songs by Heinrich Heine*, c. 1910
34: Georges Rochegrosse. Poster, 1900.
36: Leon Kroll. "Spring Romance," n.d
38: Marianne. From *Les 6 princesses*, n.d.
Back Cover: Unknown. Advertising illustration, c. 1941.

COPYRIGHT © 2010 • LAUGHING ELEPHANT BOOKS

ISBN13 978-1-59583-383-9

FIRST PRINTING • ALL RIGHTS RESERVED • PRINTED IN CHINA

www.LAUGHINGELEPHANT.com

This gathering of poems and pictures is intended as gift from one who loves to the one they love. We wish each poem to be an avowal of love, and each picture a reinforcement of the poem it accompanies.

Many great love poems do not fit into our book. Poems of grieving, poems of jealousy, poems that plead, poems of love remembered—none of these fit our criteria. We were tempted to make this an anthology of great love poems, but there are many such volumes, and we wanted something more specific; a book that said, over and over again, "I love you."

One way that literature serves us is in saying beautifully and precisely the things we have in our heart, but lack the language to express. Few of us can speak of our love with any grace or precision. This book enlists the aid of Shakespeare, Shelley, Marlowe, Elizabeth Barrett Browning and others to make our avowals.

We read many poems in gathering these, and then searched for images which would reinforce each one. Finally, we turned the text over to our designer and asked him to make a book that was the equivalent of a bouquet of flowers.

We send forth this book in the hope that it will help many people speak more eloquently the secrets of their hearts.

Here with a little Bread beneath the Bough,
A flask of wine, A Book of Verse— and Thou
Beside me singing in the Wilderness—
Oh, Wilderness were Paradise enow!

By Omar Khayyám

5

I LOVE YOU

I love you for what you are, but I
love you
yet more for what you are going to
be.
I love you not so much for your
realities
as for your ideals.
I pray for your desires that they may
be great,
rather than for your satisfactions,
which may be so hazardously little.
You are going forward toward
something great.
I am on the way with you,
and therefore I love you.

By Carl Sandburg

7

I LOVE MY LOVE

What is the meaning of the song
    That rings so clear and loud,
Thou nightingale amid the copse,
    Thou lark above the cloud?
What says thy song, thou joyous thrush,
    Up in the walnut-tree?
"I love my Love, because I know,
    My Love loves me."

What is the meaning of thy thought,
    O maiden fair and young?
There is such pleasure in thine eyes,
    Such music on thy tongue;
There is such glory on thy face—
    What can the meaning be?
"I love my Love, because I know,
    My Love loves me."

O happy words! at Beauty's feet
    We sing them ere our prime;
And when the early summers pass,
    And Care comes on with Time,
Still be it ours, in Care's despite,
    To join the chorus free—
"I love my Love, because I know,
    My Love loves me."

        By Charles Mackay

ROMANCE

I will make you brooches and toys for your delight
Of bird-song at morning and star-shine at night.
I will make a palace fit for you and me,
Of green days in forests and blue days at sea.

I will make my kitchen, and you shall keep your room,
Where white flows the river and bright blows the broom,
And you shall wash your linen and keep your body bright
In rainfall at morning and dewfall at night.

And this shall be for music when no one else is near
The fine song for singing, the rare song to hear!
That only I remember, that only you admire,
Of the broad road that stretches and the roadside fire.

By Robert Louis Stevenson

SONNET CXVI

Let me not to the marriage of true minds
Admit impediments, love is not love
Which alters when it alteration finds,
Or bends with the remover to remove.
O no! it is an ever-fixed mark,
That looks on tempests and is never shaken;
It is the star to every wand'ring bark,
Whose worth's unknown, although his height be taken.
Love's not Time's fool, though rosy lips and cheeks
Within his bending sickle's compass come,
Love alters not with his brief hours and weeks,
But bears it out even to the edge of doom:
If this be error and upon me proved,
I never writ, nor no man ever loved.

By William Shakespeare

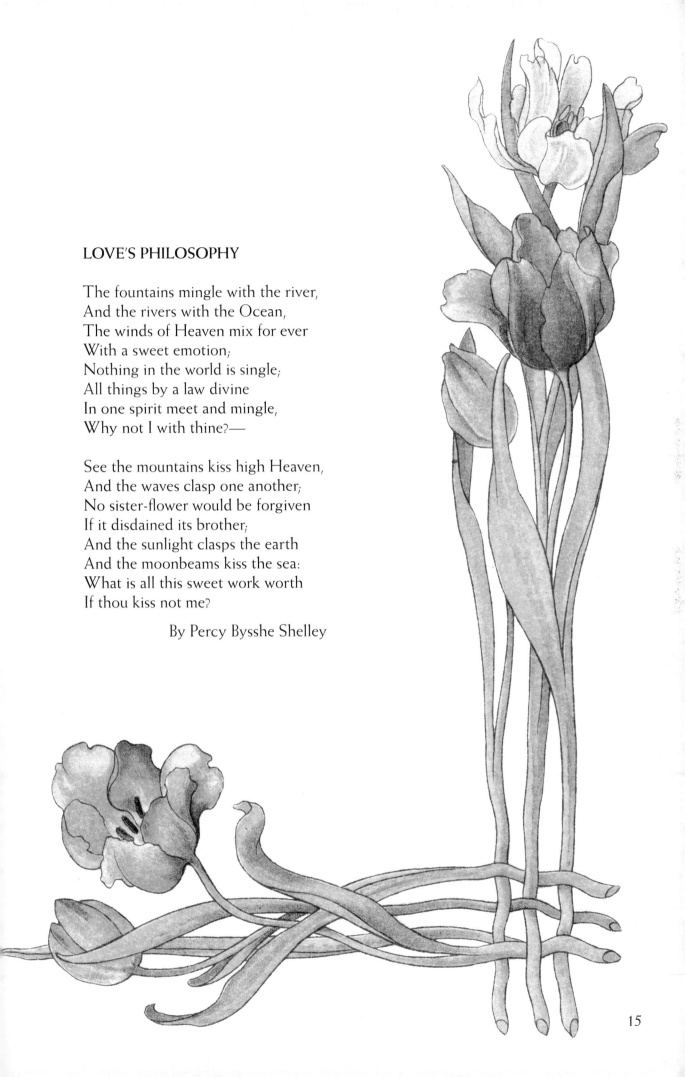

LOVE'S PHILOSOPHY

The fountains mingle with the river,
And the rivers with the Ocean,
The winds of Heaven mix for ever
With a sweet emotion;
Nothing in the world is single;
All things by a law divine
In one spirit meet and mingle,
Why not I with thine?—

See the mountains kiss high Heaven,
And the waves clasp one another;
No sister-flower would be forgiven
If it disdained its brother;
And the sunlight clasps the earth
And the moonbeams kiss the sea:
What is all this sweet work worth
If thou kiss not me?

By Percy Bysshe Shelley

15

MY DELIGHT AND THY DELIGHT

My delight and thy delight
Walking, like two angels white,
In the gardens of the night;

My desire and thy desire
Twining to a tongue of fire,
Leaping live, and laughing higher;

Through the everlasting strife
In the mystery of life.

Love, from whom the world begun,
Hath the secret of the sun.

Love can tell, and love alone,
Whence the million stars were strown,
Why each atom knows its own,
How, in spite of woe and death,
Gay is life, and sweet is breath:
This he taught us, this we knew,
Happy in his science true,
Hand in hand as we stood
'Neath the shadows of the wood,
Heart to heart as we lay
In the dawning of the day.

> By Robert Bridges

IN TIME

In time the strong and stately turrets fall,
In time the rose and silver lilies die,
In time the monarchs captive are, and thrall,
In time the sea and rivers are made dry;
The hardest flint in time doth melt asunder;
Still living fame in time doth fade away;
The mountains proud we see in time come under;
And earth, for age, we see in time decay.
The sun in time forgets for to retire
From out the east where he was wont to rise;
The basest thoughts we see in time aspire,
And greedy minds in time do wealth despise.
Thus all, sweet Fair, in time must have an end,
Except thy beauty, virtues, and thy friend.

By Giles Fletcher

THE WELCOME

Come in the evening, or come in the morning;
Come when you're looked for, or come without warning:
Kisses and welcome you'll find here before you,
And the oftener you come here the more I'll adore you!
Light is my heart since the day we were plighted;
Red is my cheek that they told me was blighted;
The green of the trees looks far greener than ever,
And the linnets are singing, "True lovers don't sever!"

I'll pull you sweet flowers, to wear if you choose them—
Or, after you've kissed them, they'll lie on my bosom;
I'll fetch from the mountain its breeze to inspire you;
I'll fetch from my fancy a tale that won't tire you.
Oh! your step's like the rain to the summer-vexed farmer,
 Or saber and shield to a knight without armor;
I'll sing you sweet songs till the stars rise above me,
Then, wandering, I'll wish you in silence to love me.

We'll look through the trees at the cliff and the eyrie;
We'll tread round the rath on the track of the fairy;
We'll look on the stars, and we'll list to the river,
Till you ask of your darling what gift you can give her:
Oh! she'll whisper you— "Love, as unchangeably beaming,
And trust, when in secret, most tunefully streaming;
Till the starlight of heaven above us shall quiver,
As our souls flow in one down eternity's river."

So come in the evening, or come in the morning;
Come when you're looked for, or come without warning:
Kisses and welcome you'll find here before you,
And the oftener you come here the more I'll adore you!
Light is my heart since the day we were plighted;
Red is my cheek that they told me was blighted;
The green of the trees looks far greener than ever,
And the linnets are singing, "True lovers don't sever!"

By Thomas Osborne Davis

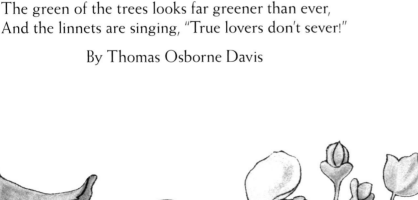

21

THE CONFIRMATION

Yes, yours, my love, is the right human face.
I in my mind had waited for this long,
Seeing the false and searching for the true,
Then found you as a traveller finds a place
Of welcome suddenly amid the wrong
Valleys and rocks and twisting roads. But you,
What shall I call you? A fountain in a waste,
A well of water in a country dry,
Or anything that's honest and good, an eye
That makes the whole world bright. Your open heart,
Simple with giving, gives the primal deed,
The first good world, the blossom, the blowing seed,
The hearth, the steadfast land, the wandering sea,
Not beautiful or rare in every part,
But like yourself, as they were meant to be.

By Edwin Muir

LOVE, WHOSE MONTH WAS EVER MAY

When with May the air is sweet,
When the forest fair is clad,
All that have a love to meet
Pair in pleasure, lass and lad.
Merrily arm in arm they go,
For the time will have it so.
Love and love, when linked together,
Love goes with to keep them gay:
All the three, this sunshine weather,
They are making holiday.
Sorrow cannot come between
Hearts where Love and May are seen.
Where to love sweet love is plighted,
Constant and with all the soul,
And the pair are so united
That their love is sound and whole:
God shall make them man and wife
For the bliss of all their life.
He that finds a constant heart,
Constant love, and constant mind,
All his sorrows shall depart.
Love, when constant, is so kind
That it makes a constant breast
Evermore content and blest.
Could I find affection true,
So sincere should be mine own:
We should conquer, being two,
Care I cannot kill alone.
Constant love is all my care:
Love inconstant I forbear.

By Sir Ulrich Von Liechtenstein

SONG TO CELIA

Drink to me only with thine eyes,
    And I will pledge with mine;
Or leave a kiss but in the cup,
    And I'll not look for wine.
The thirst that from the soul doth rise,
    Doth ask a drink divine,
But might I of Jove's nectar sip,
    I would not change for thine.

I sent thee late a rosy wreath,
    Not so much honoring thee,
As giving it a hope that there
    It could not withered be:
But thou thereon didst only breathe:
    And sent'st it back to me;
Since when it grows, and smells, I swear,
    Not of itself, but thee!

        By Ben Jonson

A RED, RED ROSE

O my luve's like a red, red rose
That's newly sprung in June:
O, my luve's like the melodie,
That's sweetly play'd in tune.

As fair art thou, my bonnie lass,
So deep in luve am I:
And I will luve thee still, my dear,
Till a' the seas gang dry.

Till a' the seas gang dry, my dear,
And the rocks melt wi' the sun:
I will luve thee still, my dear,
While the sands o' life shall run.

And fare thee weel, my only luve!
And fare thee weel a-while!
And I will come again, my luve,
Tho' it were ten thousand mile.

By Robert Burns

SONNET XLIII

How do I love thee? Let me count the ways.
I love thee to the depth and breadth and height
My soul can reach, when feeling out of sight
For the ends of Being and ideal Grace.
I love thee to the level of everyday's
Most quiet need, by sun and candle-light.
I love thee freely, as men strive for Right;
I love thee purely, as they turn from Praise.
I love thee with a passion put to use
In my old griefs, and with my childhood's faith.
I love thee with a love I seemed to lose
With my lost saints! — I love thee with the breath,
Smiles, tears, of all my life! — and, if God choose,
I shall but love thee better after death.

By Elizabeth Barrett Browning

CAPTURED

Under the elm tree where the river reaches
They watched the evening deepen in the sky,
They watched the westward clouds go towering by
Through lakes of blue toward those shining beaches,
Those far enchanted strands where blowing tides
Break into light along the shallow air:
They watched how like a tall ship's lantern there
Over that stormy surf the faint star rides.
Ship of a dream, he thought— O dreamed-of shore
Beyond all oceans and all earthly seas!
Now would they never call him any more;
Now would they never hurt him with unease.
She was that ship, that sea, that siren land,
And she was here, her hand shut in his hand.

By Archibald MacLeish

BEAUTY THAT IS NEVER OLD

When buffeted and beaten by life's storms,
When by the bitter cares of life oppressed,
I want no surer haven than your arms,
I want no sweeter heaven than your breast.

When over my life's way there falls the blight
Of sunless days, and nights of starless skies;
Enough for me, the calm and steadfast light
That softly shines within your loving eyes.

The world, for me, and all the world can hold
Is circled by your arms; for me there lies,
Within the lights and shadows of your eyes,
The only beauty that is never old.

By James Weldon Johnson

EVE SPEAKS TO ADAM

With thee conversing I forget all time,
All seasons and their change, all please alike.
Sweet is the breath of morn, her rising sweet,
With charm of earliest birds; pleasant the sun
When first on this delightful land he spreads
His orient beams, on herb, tree, fruit, and flower,
Glisetring with dew; fragrant the fertile earth
After soft showers; and sweet the coming on
Of grateful evening mild, then silent night
With this her solemn bird and this fair moon,
And these the gems of heav'n, her starry train:
But neither breath of morn when she ascends
With charm of earliest birds, nor rising sun
On this delightful land, nor herb, fruit, flower,
Glistering with dew, nor fragrance after showers,
Nor grateful evening mild, nor silent night
With this her solemn bird, nor walk by moon,
Or glittering starlight without thee is sweet.

By John Milton

37

THE PASSIONATE SHEPHERD TO HIS LOVE

Come live with me, and be my love,
And we will all the pleasures prove
That valleys, groves, hills, and fields,
Woods, or steepy mountain yields.

And we will sit upon the rocks,
Seeing the shepherds feed their flocks,
By shallow rivers to whose falls
Melodious birds sing madrigals.

And I will make thee beds of roses
And a thousand fragrant posies;
A cap of flowers, and a kirtle
Embroidered all with leaves of myrtle;

A gown made of the finest wool
Which from our pretty lambs we pull;
Fair lined slippers for the cold,
With buckles of the purest gold;

A belt of straw and ivy buds,
With coral clasps and amber studs:
And if these pleasures may thee move,
Come live with me, and be my love.

The shepherds' swains shall dance and sing
For thy delight each May morning:
If these delights thy mind may move,
Then live with me and be my love.

By Christopher Marlowe

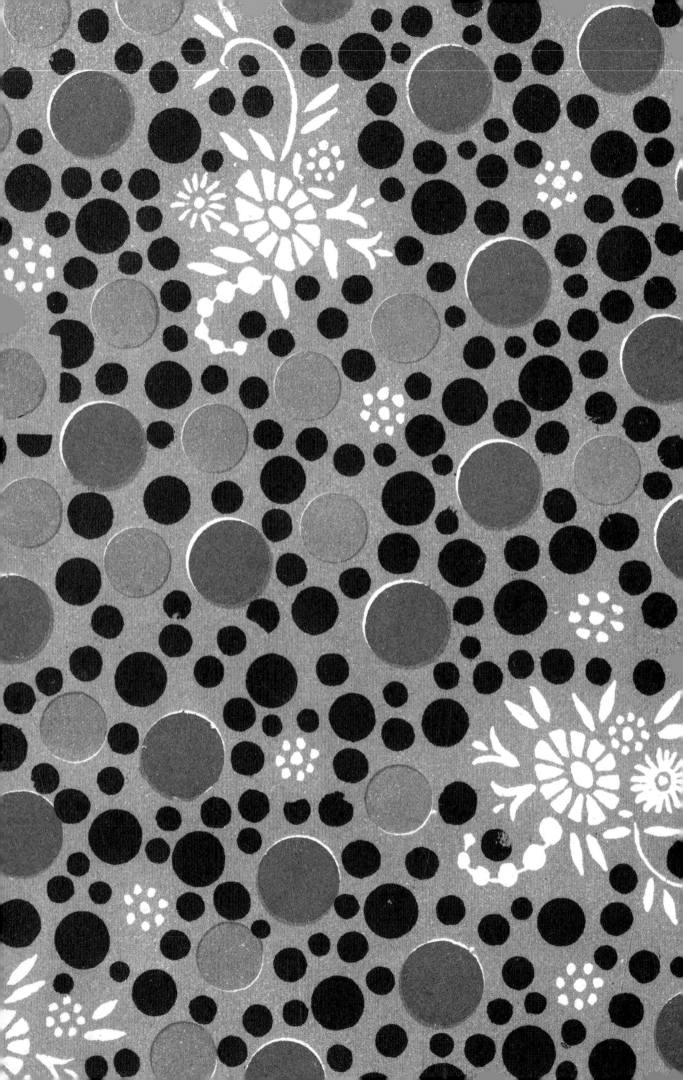